Casseroles

GALLERY BOOKS

An Imprint of W. H. Smith Publishers Inc.
112 Madison Avenue
New York City 10016

Editor: Annabel McLaren
Art editor: Caroline Dewing
Production: Richard Churchill
Illustrations and hand lettering: Ian Beck

Published by
GALLERY BOOKS
An imprint of W. H. Smith Publishers Inc.
112 Madison Avenue, New York,
New York 10016

Printed and bound in Italy

ISBN 0 8317 1802–1

Contents

Introduction

In today's busy world, few of us have the time to spend long hours preparing meals. While convenience foods are a useful standby, they are not the answer to the day-to-day task of feeding the family. Country Kitchen Casseroles – *all of which can be made in advance* – are the solution.

Nourishing, tasty combinations of meat, fish or poultry and vegetables – plus some exciting vegetarian dishes, too – are full of natural goodness. Cooked slowly in the oven or gently simmered on top of the stove, they're easy to prepare and can be economical because many use inexpensive ingredients that benefit from long, slow cooking. Not only are they tasty, they're labor-saving too – cooked in one pot, there's little washing-up afterwards!

For easy reference, we've divided the book into four sections: casseroles, ragouts, tasty topped hotpots and pot roasts. In most cases, all that's needed for an accompaniment is a side salad and hunks of crusty bread to mop up the delicious juices. If you are cooking your one pot meal in the oven you could also bake some jacket potatoes – these are always popular, especially when you are cooking for a hungry family.

Our warming one pot meals are full of country goodness, and are certain to brighten up even the gloomiest of days. Here's to happy, hearty eating!

Hearty Casseroles

Cooked slowly in the oven, casseroles need little or no attention. This gentle method of cooking – in a combination of stock and steam – not only tenderizes tougher cuts of meat and root vegetables but lets the full flavor of the dish gradually develop.

A wide variety of meats and vegetables can be casseroled. One of the most appealing aspects of the method is the way unusual ingredients can be combined with delicious results – apricots and almonds cooked with beef make for a spicy stew with a fruity flavor; chunks of lean turkey simmered with leeks, fennel, cauliflower and walnuts make a delicately-flavored dish with a creamy sauce.

Veal & pepper pot

Serves 8

¾ cup all-purpose flour
salt and freshly ground black pepper
4½ lb stew veal, trimmed of fat and cut in 1 inch cubes
¼ cup margarine or butter
3 tablespoons vegetable oil
2 large onions, chopped
3 celery stalks, chopped
3 sweet red peppers, seeded and sliced
1¼ cups medium-dry white wine
2½ cups water
2 chicken bouillon cubes
1 teaspoon dried marjoram
¾ cup pitted ripe olives
FOR GARNISH
4 tablespoons chopped fresh parsley
finely grated rind of 1 large lemon

1 Preheat the oven to 350°F.

2 Put the flour in a plastic bag and season with salt and pepper. Place the meat in the bag and shake until the meat is well coated with flour. Reserve excess flour.

3 Heat the margarine and oil in a large Dutch oven, add half the meat and sauté over brisk heat, turning it until sealed on all sides without browning. Remove from pot with a slotted spoon and set aside. Fry the remaining meat and remove with a slotted spoon.

4 Add the onions, celery and peppers to the pot, cover and cook gently over low heat for 10 minutes, stirring the ingredients well from time to time.

5 Sprinkle the reserved seasoned flour into the pot, stir well and cook for 1 minute.

6 Pour in the wine and water and bring to a boil, stirring frequently. Crumble in the bouillon cubes and add the marjoram, then return the meat to the pot and bring slowly back to a boil, stirring occasionally.

7 Cover the pot and cook in the oven for 2 hours. Remove from the oven, taste and adjust the seasoning and stir in the olives.

8 Mix the parsley with the lemon rind, then sprinkle it over the top of the casserole and serve at once.

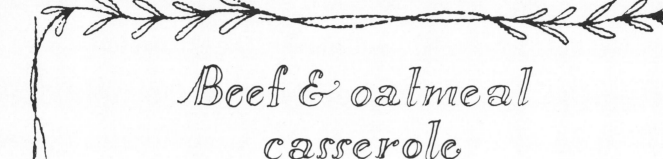

Beef & oatmeal casserole

Serves 4

¼ cup vegetable oil
2 onions, thinly sliced
3 tablespoons fine oatmeal
salt and freshly ground black pepper
1 lb lean stew beef, trimmed of excess fat and cut in 1 inch cubes
1 teaspoon Savita
1¼ cups boiling water
1½ packages (10 oz size) frozen mixed vegetables

1 Preheat the oven to 325°F.
2 Heat half the oil in a skillet. Add the onions and sauté gently for 5 minutes until soft and lightly colored. Using a slotted spoon, transfer the onions to a Dutch oven.
3 Put the oatmeal in a plastic bag and season with salt and pepper. Add the beef cubes and shake well to coat the meat thoroughly in the seasoned oatmeal.
4 Heat the remaining oil in the skillet, add the coated beef cubes and cook briskly for a few minutes, stirring until sealed and brown. Using a slotted spoon, transfer the brown beef cubes to the pot.
5 Mix together the Savita and water and pour into the skillet. Bring to a boil, stirring constantly with a wooden spoon to scrape up the sediment from the base of the pan. Pour the mixture over the onions and beef contained in the pot.
6 Cover the casserole and cook in the oven for 1½ hours. Add the mixed vegetables and cook for 30 minutes more or until the beef is tender when pierced with a sharp knife. Serve the stew hot, straight from the pot.

Old~time tea~pot

Serves 4

1 tablespoon oil
2 large onions, chopped
4 carrots, sliced
¼ cup flour
salt and freshly ground black pepper
1½ lb lean chuck steak, cut in small cubes
2 tablespoons butter, more if necessary
2½ cups strong tea
1 tablespoon tomato paste
1 teaspoon dried mixed herbs
4 beef bouillon cubes, crumbled
1 cup sliced mushrooms

1 Preheat the oven to 300°F. In a skillet, heat the oil and sauté the onions and carrots for 3 minutes. Using a slotted spoon, transfer them to a casserole.

2 Put the flour in a plastic bag and season with salt and pepper. Add the beef cubes and shake to coat them thoroughly. Add 2 tablespoons butter to the skillet and, when it is hot, add the meat and brown lightly. Transfer the meat to the casserole with a slotted spoon. Add any remaining flour to the pan, adding more butter if necessary, and cook briefly.

3 Stir in the tea and bring to a boil, add the tomato paste, herbs, bouillon cubes and salt and pepper to taste and pour into the casserole. Add the mushrooms, stir, cover and cook in the oven for 2 hours, or until the meat is tender when pierced with a sharp knife, then transfer to a heated serving dish, if wished, and serve.

Apricot & almond beef

Serves 4

1 tablespoon vegetable oil
2 small onions, sliced
3 tablespoons all-purpose flour
salt and freshly ground black pepper
1½ lb top round steak, cut in 1 inch cubes
1 tablespoon prepared English mustard
1 tablespoon molasses
1 tablespoon tomato paste
1¼ cups beef stock
1 cup dried apricots, soaked overnight in ⅔ cup hard cider
2 large carrots, sliced
2 celery stalks, thinly sliced
½ cup slivered almonds, lightly toasted

1 Preheat the oven to 325°F.
2 Heat the oil in a Dutch oven, add the onions and cook gently for 5 minutes until soft and lightly colored.
3 Put the flour in a plastic bag and season with salt and pepper. Add the meat cubes and shake to coat them thoroughly. Reserve any excess seasoned flour.
4 Add the meat cubes to the pot and sauté them briskly for 2–3 minutes, to seal the meat. Remove from the heat.
5 In a bowl, mix together the mustard, molasses, tomato paste and stock. Stir into the pot. Drain the cider from the soaked apricots and stir into the pot with the reserved seasoned flour.
6 Chop the apricots in small pieces and add to the pot with the carrots and celery.
7 Return to the heat and bring to a boil, then reduce the heat and simmer for 2–3 minutes, stirring.
8 Cover and cook in the oven for about 2 hours or until the meat and vegetables are tender when pierced with a sharp knife.
9 Stir half the toasted almonds into the pot, then taste and adjust the seasoning, if necessary. Serve at once, straight from the pot, with the remaining almonds sprinkled on top.

Rosemary lamb casserole

Serves 4–6

2 tablespoons all-purpose flour
2 tablespoons chopped fresh rosemary, or 2 teaspoons crushed dried rosemary
salt and freshly ground black pepper
3–3½ lb boneless lean lamb shoulder, trimmed of excess fat and cut in 1 inch cubes
¼ cup vegetable oil
2 onions, roughly chopped
1½ cups sliced carrots
1¼ cups chicken stock
rosemary sprigs, for garnish

1 Preheat the oven to 325°F.
2 Put the flour in a plastic bag and add the rosemary and salt and pepper to taste. Add the lamb cubes and shake to coat thoroughly.
3 Heat half the oil in a large Dutch oven, add the onions and carrots and sauté over moderate heat for 3 minutes, stirring. Remove the vegetables from the pot with a slotted spoon and drain thoroughly on kitchen paper towels.
4 Heat the remaining oil in the pot, add the lamb and cook over brisk heat for 2–3 minutes, stirring, until browned all over. Return the onions and carrots to the Dutch oven, pour in the stock and bring to a boil, scraping the sediment from the base and side of the pot with a wooden spoon.
5 Cover and cook in the oven for 2 hours, until the lamb is tender when pierced with a sharp knife. Garnish the lamb casserole with the rosemary sprigs and serve it at once straight from the pot.

Shepherd's delight

Serves 4

2 breasts of lamb, total weight around 2 lb, trimmed and jointed
1–2 tablespoons vegetable oil
2 onions, chopped
1 large clove garlic, crushed (optional)
1 can (16 oz) tomatoes
3 tablespoons tomato paste
1 cup black-eyed peas, soaked in fresh cold water for 12 hours and drained
2 teaspoons fresh marjoram or 1 teaspoon dried marjoram
⅔–1¼ cups chicken stock
salt and freshly ground black pepper

1 Preheat the oven to 350°F.
2 Cut the trimmed breasts into 6 or 8 strips parallel with the bones.
3 Heat 1 tablespoon oil in a large Dutch oven. Add the lamb in 1 or 2 batches and sauté over moderate heat for 5–10 minutes until golden on all sides. Remove with a slotted spoon and set aside.
4 Add another tablespoon of oil to the pot, if necessary, then add the onions and garlic, if using, and cook gently for about 5 minutes until lightly colored.
5 Stir in the canned tomatoes with their juice, breaking the tomatoes up a little with a wooden spoon. Stir in the tomato paste, drained peas and fresh or dried marjoram.

6 Add the lamb to the pea mixture, distributing it evenly, then top up with enough stock just to cover the meat. Add pepper to taste, then cover tightly and cook in the oven for about 2½ hours until both lamb and peas are tender. Check the pot occasionally and top up with extra stock or water if necessary.
7 When the meat and peas are cooked, remove the pot from the oven and blot any excess fat from the surface with kitchen paper towels, or otherwise you may remove it with a bulb baster.
8 To complete the dish, add salt and pepper to taste, then serve hot, straight from the pot.

Rich braised oxtail

Serves 4

3 tablespoons oil
3¼ lb oxtail pieces
2 cups sliced carrots
1 large onion, sliced
2 cups parsnips, in chunks
1 tablespoon Graham flour
2½ cups beef stock
2 tablespoons ketchup
¼ cup red wine
bouquet garni
salt and freshly ground black pepper

1 Preheat the oven to 300°F.
2 Heat the oil in a fairly large Dutch oven, add the oxtail pieces and sauté over brisk heat until brown on all sides. With a slotted spoon remove the oxtail pieces and set aside.
3 Pour off all but 1½ tablespoons fat from the pot. Add the vegetables, reduce the heat and sauté them gently for about 10 minutes. Sprinkle in the flour and stir until absorbed.

4 Return the oxtail to the pot with the stock, ketchup, wine and the bouquet garni. Add salt and pepper to taste.
5 Cover the pot with foil, then add the lid, and cook in the oven for 3–3½ hours until the oxtail is very tender and the meat comes away easily from the bones. Discard the bouquet garni, then taste and adjust the seasoning of the sauce. Serve at once, straight from the Dutch oven.

Farmhouse chicken & hog jowl

Serves 4

¼ cup all-purpose flour
salt and freshly ground white pepper
4 chicken parts, each weighing 9–10 oz
½ lb piece country-cured hog jowl, finely diced
1 small head celery, finely chopped
2 medium-size onions, minced
butter or shortening, for greasing
½ teaspoon dried sage
½ teaspoon dried thyme
1¼ cups milk
½ cup strong chicken stock

1 Preheat the oven to 325°F. Put the flour in a plastic bag and season with salt and pepper. Add the chicken parts and shake to coat them thoroughly. Remove the chicken parts from the bag, shaking off excess flour. Add the hog jowl to the bag and coat the pieces in the same way.

2 Put half the celery and onion in the base of a greased casserole. Arrange the chicken portions on top and cover with the hog jowl. Sprinkle in the herbs, then add the rest of the celery and onion. Mix the milk and stock and pour over the ingredients in the pot.

3 Cover and cook in the oven for 2½ hours. Serve hot, straight from the casserole.

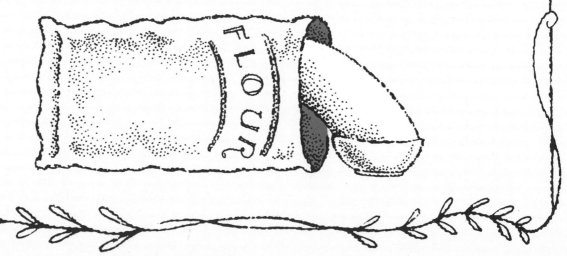

Honeyed orange pork

Serves 4

2 large oranges
2 tablespoons all-purpose flour
salt and freshly ground black pepper
1½ lb lean boneless pork loin, trimmed of excess fat and cut in 1 inch cubes
2 tablespoons margarine or butter
1 tablespoon vegetable oil
1 onion, minced
2 tablespoons honey
2 cloves garlic, crushed (optional)
1¼ cups chicken stock
watercress sprigs, for garnish

1 Finely grate the rind from half an orange, then peel and section the oranges and remove the pith completely. Reserve.

2 Place the flour in a plastic bag and season with salt and pepper. Add the pork cubes and shake until well coated, then remove from the bag and set aside. Reserve any excess seasoned flour.

3 Heat the margarine and oil in a Dutch oven. Add the onion and sauté gently for 5 minutes until soft and lightly colored. Stir in the honey, add the pork cubes and sauté over moderate heat for 10–15 minutes, stirring often until well browned on all sides.

4 Meanwhile, preheat the oven to 350°F.

5 Add any reserved seasoned flour to the pot, with the orange rind and garlic, if using. Sauté for 5 minutes, then stir in the chicken stock and bring to a boil, stirring constantly with a wooden spoon.

6 Cover the pot and cook in the oven for 1½–1¾ hours, stirring occasionally, until the pork is tender when it is pierced with a sharp knife.

7 Remove from the oven, taste and adjust seasoning if necessary and stir in the orange sections. Cover again and let stand for 5 minutes, then stir again.

8 To complete the dish, garnish with the watercress sprigs and then serve the casserole at once, straight from the pot.

Country turkey

Serves 4–6

2 tablespoons margarine or butter
1¾ lb boneless turkey, skin removed and cut in bite-size pieces
¼ cup all-purpose flour
⅔ cup chicken stock
1¼ cups milk
3 leeks, cut in ½ inch slices
⅔ cup thinly sliced fennel
1 bay leaf
½ small cauliflower, divided into flowerets
¼ cup roughly chopped walnuts
good pinch of celery salt
freshly ground black pepper
fennel tops, for garnish

1 Preheat the oven to 350°F.
2 Melt the margarine in a large skillet, add half the turkey and cook over moderate heat for about 5 minutes, stirring occasionally, until browned on all sides. Remove the turkey with a slotted spoon and transfer to a large casserole.
3 Add the remaining turkey to the pan and brown on all sides in the same way. Remove with a slotted spoon and transfer to the casserole.
4 Sprinkle the flour into the fat remaining in the skillet and stir over low heat for 1–2 minutes. Off heat, gradually stir in the stock and milk. Return to the heat and simmer, stirring, until thick and smooth.
5 Pour the sauce over the turkey in the casserole. Add the leeks, fennel and bay leaf and stir well to mix.
6 Cover the casserole and cook in the oven for 30 minutes or until the turkey is almost tender. Stir in the cauliflower flowerets and walnuts and cook for a further 30–40 minutes until the cauliflower is tender and the turkey cooked through.
7 Remove the bay leaf and season the casserole with celery salt and pepper to taste. Garnish with fennel tops and serve hot, straight from the dish.

Chicken casserole

Serves 4

2 large potatoes, quartered
salt and freshly ground black pepper
4 chicken parts, each weighing 9–10 oz
½ cup all-purpose flour
3 tablespoons vegetable oil
1 small onion, chopped
4 bacon slices, cut in strips
½ cup halved button mushrooms
2 cups chicken stock
1 tablespoon minced fresh parsley

1 Bring the potatoes to a boil in salted water, reduce heat and simmer for 10 minutes.

2 Meanwhile, pat the chicken parts dry with kitchen paper towels. Put the flour in a plastic bag and season with salt and pepper. Place the chicken parts in the bag and shake until well coated. Reserve the excess flour.

3 Preheat the oven to 375°F.

4 Heat 2 tablespoons of the oil in a large skillet, add the chicken parts and sauté for 4–5 minutes on each side, until golden brown.

5 Transfer the chicken parts to a large casserole with a slotted spoon. Drain the potatoes and arrange them around the chicken parts.

6 Heat the remaining oil in the skillet. Add the onion, bacon and mushrooms and sauté gently for 5 minutes until the onion is soft. Transfer the vegetables and bacon to the casserole.

7 Sprinkle the reserved seasoned flour into the skillet and cook over gentle heat, stirring, for 1–2 minutes. Gradually stir in the stock, then bring to a boil, stirring. Stir in the parsley, then pour the hot mixture into the casserole.

8 Cover the casserole and cook in the oven for 1–1¼ hours, until the chicken is cooked (the juices run clear when the chicken is pierced in the thickest part with a fine skewer). Serve at once, straight from the casserole.

Casseroled barley & bacon

Serves 4

2 tablespoons margarine or butter
10 bacon slices, finely chopped
2 large onions, thinly sliced
1½ cups thinly sliced carrots
1 cup chopped celery
1 cup thinly sliced mushrooms
1¼ cups pearl barley
2½ cups chicken stock
4 tablespoons chopped fresh parsley
salt and freshly ground black pepper

1 Preheat the oven to 350°F.
2 Melt the margarine in a Dutch oven. Add the bacon and onions and sauté gently for 5 minutes until the onions are soft and lightly colored.
3 Stir in the carrots, celery, mushrooms and pearl barley, then pour in the stock and bring to a boil. Add the parsley and salt and pepper to taste.
4 Cover the pot and cook in the oven for 1 hour, or until the barley is soft and the liquid absorbed. Serve hot.

Liver casserole

Serves 4

5 bacon slices, cut in strips
1 lb beef liver, cut in ¼ inch thick slices
2 tablespoons margarine or butter
1 onion, chopped
1 green pepper, seeded and thinly sliced
1 can (16 oz) tomatoes
salt and freshly ground black pepper
1 teaspoon chopped fresh thyme, or ½ teaspoon dried thyme

1 Preheat the oven to 350°F.
2 Arrange the bacon strips on the base of a casserole, and place the liver slices on top of the bacon.
3 Melt the margarine in a skillet, add the onion and green pepper and cook very gently for 5 minutes until the onion is soft and lightly colored. Remove onion and green pepper with a slotted spoon and scatter over the liver. Add tomatoes with their juice, then season the casserole with salt, pepper and the fresh chopped or dried thyme.
4 Cover the casserole and cook in the oven for 1½ hours or until the liver is tender when pierced with a knife. Taste and adjust seasoning if necessary. Serve at once, straight from the casserole.

Boston baked chicken

Serves 4

8 chicken drumsticks, skinned
1 can (16 oz) pinto beans, drained
1 cup fresh tomato sauce
1 tablespoon molasses
½ teaspoon dry mustard
½ cup chicken stock
1 large onion, thinly sliced
1 small green pepper, seeded and roughly chopped
salt and freshly ground black pepper
FOR GARNISH
½ teaspoon mild paprika
green and sweet red pepper rings (optional)

1 Preheat the oven to 375°F.
2 Place the skinned chicken drumsticks in a large ovenproof dish.
3 In a bowl, mix together the remaining ingredients and season to taste with salt and pepper. Mix thoroughly, then spoon the mixture over the chicken drumsticks.
4 Cover and cook in the oven for 1–1¼ hours, stirring occasionally, until the chicken is tender and juices run clear when the meat is pierced in the thickest part of the flesh with a sharp knife or fine skewer.
5 Let cool for 5 minutes, then sprinkle with paprika and garnish with the green and sweet red pepper rings, if liked. Serve at once, piping hot.

Rich Ragouts

Ragouts – or stews – are gently simmered on top of the range, the ingredients cooking in a rich stock which may be pepped up with a glass of wine or a dash of brandy.

Our ragouts range from homely stews with dumplings to classic Blanquette of lamb and delicious seafood suppers. The ingredients usually require a shorter cooking time than casseroles which are cooked in the oven; like casseroles, the flavor is even more pronounced if you cook one day and reheat the next.

If you are a potato addict, add pared, even-size chunks to any of the recipes for an even more substantial dish.

Beef stew

Serves 4

¼ cup all-purpose flour
salt and freshly ground black pepper
1½ lb chuck steak, trimmed of fat and cut in 1 inch cubes
2 tablespoons margarine or butter
2 tablespoons vegetable oil
1 onion, roughly chopped
2 large carrots, thinly sliced
2 celery stalks, thinly sliced
2 teaspoons tomato paste
2 teaspoons minced parsley
pinch of cayenne
1¼ cups beef stock
juice of 1 orange
DUMPLINGS
1 cup self-rising flour
salt
¼ cup chopped suet
1 tablespoon minced parsley
1 teaspoon dried mixed herbs
about ¼ cup water

1 Put the flour in a plastic bag, season with salt and pepper, then add the meat. Shake the bag vigorously until the meat is well coated.

2 Heat the margarine and 1 tablespoon oil in a large Dutch oven. Add the meat and sauté over brisk heat for about 3 minutes, stirring, until browned on all sides. Cook the meat in batches if necessary. Remove from the pot with a slotted spoon and set aside.

3 Heat the remaining oil in the pot, then add the onion, carrots and celery and sauté over moderate heat for 3 minutes. Return the meat to the pot, then add the remaining ingredients.

4 Bring to a boil, stirring and scraping up all the sediment from the side and bottom of the pot. Lower the heat, cover and simmer for 1½–2 hours until the meat is tender.

5 About 10 minutes before the end of the cooking time, prepare the dumplings: Sift the flour and a pinch of salt into a bowl and stir in the suet, parsley and herbs. With a round-bladed knife, gradually stir in the water to mix to a soft but not sticky dough. Knead the dough lightly, then form into 8 balls.

6 Taste and adjust the seasoning of the stew, then place the dumplings on top. Cover and simmer for 15 minutes until the dumplings are puffed up. Serve at once, straight from the pot.

Beef & pumpkin ragout

Serves 4–6

3 tablespoons margarine or butter
2 onions, sliced
2 cloves garlic, minced
1 large green pepper, seeded and finely chopped
1½ lb chuck steak, cut in 1½ inch cubes
4 bacon slices, chopped
1 cup red wine
salt and freshly ground black pepper
1 lb pumpkin, pared and cut in 1½ inch cubes

1 Melt the margarine in a large Dutch oven. Add onions, garlic and green pepper and cook gently for 5 minutes.
2 Increase the heat slightly, add the meat and bacon and cook, turning, to brown the meat on all sides.
3 Stir in the wine and season with salt and pepper. Bring to a boil, lower the heat, cover and simmer for 5 minutes.
5 Add the pumpkin to the pot, bring back to a boil, then lower the heat, cover and simmer gently for 1½–2 hours, until the meat is tender when pierced with a sharp knife. Taste and adjust seasoning. Serve the ragout at once straight from the pot.

Pork medley

Serves 4

2 tablespoons vegetable oil
1 onion, chopped
½ lb lean pork tenderloin, cut in 1 inch cubes
4 lamb kidneys, halved and cores removed
¾ lb tomatoes, peeled and quartered
3 tablespoons sweet red vermouth
½ teaspoon dried oregano
salt and freshly ground black pepper
⅔ cup plain yogurt

1 Heat the oil in a large kettle, then add the onion and sauté very gently for 5 minutes until soft and lightly colored.

2 Add the pork to the kettle and sauté, turning from time to time, for 10 minutes until lightly browned.

3 Cut each kidney half in 4 pieces. Add to the kettle and sauté, stirring frequently, for 5 minutes.

4 Stir in the tomatoes, vermouth and oregano, and season to taste with salt and pepper. Cover and cook for 10 minutes, then remove the lid and cook for a further 5 minutes until the pork is tender when pierced with a sharp knife.

5 Remove from the heat, taste and adjust seasoning, then swirl in the plain yogurt. Spoon the Pork medley into a warmed serving dish and serve at once.

Pork & sweet potato stew

Serves 4

2 tablespoons shortening
2 lb fresh picnic shoulder of pork, cut in ¾ inch dice
2 medium-size onions, sliced
1 garlic clove, minced
2 large sweet red peppers, seeded and cut in strips
1 tablespoon mild paprika
¼ teaspoon cayenne
1 lb tomatoes, blanched, peeled and chopped
⅔ cup dry white wine
⅔ cup chicken stock
1½ lb sweet potatoes, pared and cut in ¾ inch dice
6 sage leaves
salt

1 Melt the shortening in a large kettle on a high heat. Add the diced pork, brown it quickly and remove it from the pan with a slotted spoon. Lower the heat. Add the onions and garlic and cook them until they are soft.

2 Add the peppers, cover and cook for 5 minutes. Stir in the paprika and cayenne. Add the tomatoes, cover and cook for 5 minutes more, until they are very soft.

3 Pour in the wine and stock and bring to a boil. Add the pork, sweet potatoes and sage and season with salt. Cover the kettle and cook on a low heat for 45 minutes. Serve at once.

Blanquette of Lamb

Serves 4

2 tablespoons vegetable oil
2 large onions, sliced
2 carrots, diced
1¼ lb lamb leg steaks, cut in ¾ inch cubes
1 cup quartered button mushrooms
about 2½ cups water
bouquet garni
salt and freshly ground black pepper
1 tablespoon all-purpose flour
⅔ cup frozen peas
⅓ cup frozen whole kernel corn
1 tablespoon chopped chives, for garnish

1 Heat the oil in a Dutch oven, add the onions and sauté for 1–2 minutes. Add the carrots, lamb cubes and mushrooms. Sauté for 2–3 minutes more, stirring.

2 Pour in just enough water to cover the lamb and vegetables. Add the bouquet garni, season with salt and pepper and bring to a boil. Lower the heat, cover and simmer very gently for 1½ hours.

3 In a small bowl, mix the flour to a smooth paste with a little cold water. Add 3–4 tablespoons of hot cooking liquid, stir well, then stir the mixture into the pot.

4 Add the peas and corn and return to a boil, stirring constantly. Lower the heat and simmer for a further 8–10 minutes, until tender.

5 Discard the bouquet garni, taste and adjust seasoning, then sprinkle the lamb with chives. Serve at once, straight from the pot.

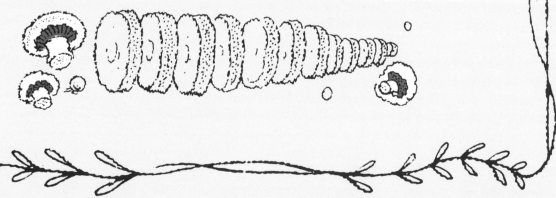

Veal & vegetable ragout

Serves 4

1½ lb pie veal, trimmed and cut in 1 inch cubes
¼ cup all-purpose flour
1 teaspoon garlic salt
freshly ground black pepper
¼ cup margarine or butter
4 carrots, sliced
4 celery stalks, sliced
1 tablespoon mild paprika
1 can (16 oz) chopped tomatoes
1¼ cups chicken stock
¼ lb button mushrooms
⅔ cup dairy sour cream

1 Put the veal in a saucepan and pour in enough cold water just to cover. Bring to a boil, then strain. Rinse the foam from the veal under cold running water, then pat the meat dry with kitchen paper towels.

2 Put the flour, garlic salt and plenty of pepper in a plastic bag. Add the veal cubes and shake until they are evenly coated. Reserve any excess seasoned flour.

3 Melt the margarine in a large heavy-bottomed kettle or Dutch oven, add the veal and sauté over brisk heat, stirring until the veal is sealed on all sides. Add the carrots and celery and cook for 2 minutes, stirring. Sprinkle in the paprika and reserved seasoned flour, stir well.

4 Pour in the canned tomatoes with their juice and the stock and bring to a boil, stirring frequently. Lower heat, cover kettle and simmer for 40 minutes or until meat is tender.

5 Stir in the mushrooms, cover again and cook for 20 minutes.

6 Off heat, stir in half the cream, then taste and adjust seasoning. Reheat very gently. Do not let boil. Serve at once, in a warmed casserole if the stew was cooked in a kettle, with the remaining cream swirled on top.

Spicy lamb

Serves 4

2 tablespoons vegetable oil
1 onion, chopped
1½ lb lamb leg steaks, trimmed of excess fat and cut in 1 inch cubes
½ teaspoon ground ginger
¼ teaspoon ground cinnamon
2½ cups chicken stock
⅔ cup pitted prunes, soaked for 2 hours in boiling water
2 crisp dessert apples
1 tablespoon honey

1 Heat the oil in a large Dutch oven, add the onion and sauté over moderate heat for 2 minutes, stirring. Add the lamb, increase the heat and sauté for 2 minutes, stirring, until the lamb is evenly browned.

2 Sprinkle in ginger and cinnamon, stir in the stock and bring to a boil. Lower the heat, cover the pot and simmer gently for 1½ hours, until the meat is tender.

3 Drain the prunes. Pare, quarter and core the apples and slice them fairly thickly. Add to the pot with the drained prunes and honey. Stir well, cover and simmer for a further 20 minutes, until the meat is tender and the fruit soft. Serve immediately.

Sausage pot

Serves 4–6

4½ cups shredded red cabbage
1 onion, chopped
1 tart apple, pared, cored and sliced
1 clove garlic, minced (optional)
½ teaspoon caraway seeds
1½ teaspoons sugar
⅔–1¼ cups chicken stock or white wine
2 tablespoons red wine vinegar
salt and freshly ground black pepper
½ lb cooked spicy sausage, skinned and chopped or sliced
¼–⅓ cup plain yogurt or dairy sour cream, to serve

1 Put the cabbage in a Dutch oven with the onion, apple, garlic, if using, caraway seeds and sugar. Pour in ⅔ cup of the stock or wine and the vinegar and season well with salt and pepper. Mix all the ingredients thoroughly in the pot.

2 Bring to a boil, then lower the heat, cover and simmer for about 1 hour, stirring occasionally until the cabbage is very tender. Add a little more stock during cooking, if necessary.

3 Add the sausage to the pot and cook for 5–10 minutes more.

4 Serve hot, straight from the Dutch oven, swirling a spoonful of plain yogurt or dairy sour cream onto each of the servings.

Atlantic supper

Serves 6

3 tablespoons olive or sunflower oil
2 onions, chopped
2 cloves garlic, minced
4 scallions, chopped
1 green pepper, seeded and chopped
4 tablespoons minced fresh parsley
⅔ cup dry white wine
⅔ cup water
1 can (16 oz) chopped tomatoes
4 tablespoons tomato paste
2 tablespoons brandy (optional)
salt and freshly ground black pepper
2 lb haddock fillets, skinned and cut in 2 inch pieces
1 cup shelled shrimp
12 cooked shrimp in shells, for garnish

1 Heat the oil in a Dutch oven, add the onions and garlic and sauté over moderate heat for 10 minutes until browned.

2 Add the scallions, green pepper and half the parsley, stir well and sauté for 5 minutes.

3 Mix the wine with the water and add to the pot, together with the chopped tomatoes, tomato paste and brandy, if using. Cook for 2 minutes to allow the alcohol to evaporate, then season to taste with salt and pepper. Add the haddock chunks and shelled shrimp to the pot and stir gently to mix the ingredients.

4 Cover the pot and continue to cook over moderate heat for 15 minutes, until the haddock flakes easily. Off heat, garnish with the shrimp in shells and serve at once, straight from the Dutch oven.

Chicken & peanut stew

Serves 4

1 broiler-fryer, weighing 3–3½ lb, thoroughly thawed if frozen, jointed
into 8 parts and skinned
2 onions, chopped
salt and freshly ground black pepper
½ lb fresh okra, washed and stem ends trimmed
¼ cup malt vinegar
1¼ cups roasted peanuts
¼ cup peanut oil
2–3 fresh chilis, minced
1 can (8 oz) chopped tomatoes
1 tablespoon tomato paste
4 hard-cooked eggs, shelled but left whole

1 Put the chicken parts in a large kettle with half the onion. Pour in fresh cold water to cover and season with salt and pepper. Bring slowly to a boil, skim if necessary, then lower heat, cover and cook for 30 minutes, until the chicken parts are just cooked through (the juices run clear when pierced in the thickest part with a fine skewer).

2 Meanwhile, put the okra in a bowl, pour in cold water to cover and add the vinegar. Let soak. Work the nuts in a food processor or coffee grinder for a few seconds until reduced to a coarse paste. Set aside.

3 Transfer the cooked chicken to a large Dutch oven with a slotted spoon. Set aside. Strain 2½ cups cooking liquid into a liquid measure.

4 Heat 3 tablespoons of the oil in a saucepan. Add the remaining onion and the chilis and sauté gently for 5 minutes, until the onion is soft and lightly colored. Off heat, add the peanut paste, then gradually stir in the measured cooking liquid from the chicken. Stir in the tomatoes with their juice and the tomato paste. Taste and adjust the seasoning if necessary.

5 Pour over the chicken parts and turn to coat in the sauce. Cover and let stand for 1 hour. Set the pot over gentle heat on top of the range and reheat for 15 minutes, stirring from time to time.

6 Drain the okra. Heat remaining oil in a saucepan, add the okra and cook gently, turning occasionally, for 5 minutes. Using a slotted spoon, transfer the okra to the pot and add the eggs. Place over very gentle heat for 15 minutes more, then taste and adjust the seasoning. Serve at once.

Bosun's bowl

Serves 4

2 tablespoons vegetable oil
3 bacon slices, chopped
1½ lb cod fillets, skinned and cut in 1 inch cubes
1 onion, chopped
1 clove garlic, minced (optional)
1 lb potatoes, cut in ½ inch dice
1 can (16 oz) chopped tomatoes
2 cups chicken stock
2 tablespoons minced fresh parsley
1 bay leaf
1 teaspoon mild paprika
2 teaspoons capers, rinsed
salt and freshly ground black pepper
1 cup shelled shrimp, thawed if frozen (optional)
a little extra minced fresh parsley and mild paprika, for garnish

1 Heat the oil in a Dutch oven, add the bacon and sauté gently for 2–3 minutes until the fat runs. Remove the bacon with a slotted spoon and reserve.

2 Add the fish cubes to the pot and cook briskly, turning carefully once or twice, for 2 minutes or until lightly browned and opaque. Remove the fish carefully with a slotted spoon and reserve.

3 Return the reserved bacon to the pot and add the onion and garlic, if using. Cook gently for 5 minutes until the onion is soft and lightly colored. Add the potatoes and cook for 1 further minute.

4 Add the tomatoes, stock, parsley, bay leaf, paprika and capers to the pot. Stir well to mix and season to taste with salt and pepper. Bring to a boil, then lower heat, cover and simmer gently for 20 minutes or until the potatoes are tender when pierced with a knife.

5 Add the cooked fish and shrimp, if using, to the pot, stir very carefully and heat gently for 2–3 minutes. Taste and adjust the seasoning, if necessary.

6 Transfer the contents of the Dutch oven to a warmed deep serving bowl, sprinkle with the minced fresh parsley and the mild paprika to garnish and serve at once.

Chili beans

Serves 4

2 tablespoons vegetable oil
2 onions, minced
1 sweet red pepper, seeded and cut in 2 × ½ inch strips
1 clove garlic, minced
2 cups ground beef
¼ cup all-purpose flour
1 teaspoon chili powder
1 teaspoon ground cumin
1 teaspoon dried oregano
1 tablespoon tomato paste
1 can (8 oz) tomatoes
1¼ cups beef stock
salt
1 can (16 oz) cannellini beans, drained and rinsed

1 Heat the oil in a large heavy-bottomed skillet, add the onions, sweet red pepper and garlic, and sauté gently for 5 minutes until the onion and pepper are soft.

2 Add the ground beef, raise the heat to high and cook until the meat is evenly browned, stirring with a wooden spoon to remove lumps.

3 Off heat, stir in the flour, chili powder, cumin and oregano. Add the tomato paste, the tomatoes with their juice and the beef stock.

4 Return to the heat and bring to a boil, stirring. Season with salt but not with pepper. Cover the pan, lower the heat and simmer the contents for 40 minutes.

5 Stir in the cannellini beans and simmer for a further 5 minutes to heat through. Spoon into a warmed serving dish and serve at once.

Cottage~style lentils

Serves 4

1 tablespoon vegetable oil
1 large onion, thinly sliced
4 cups chicken stock
1¼ cups split red lentils
1 lb potatoes, cut in even-size chunks
4 tomatoes, peeled, quartered and seeded
½ teaspoon dried marjoram or thyme
½ teaspoon mild paprika
salt and freshly ground black pepper
⅔ cup frozen peas
1 cup thinly sliced button mushrooms

1 Heat the oil in a large kettle, add the onion and sauté over moderate heat for 3–4 minutes, stirring occasionally.
2 Add the stock to the kettle and bring to a boil. Add the lentils, potatoes, tomatoes, herbs, paprika and salt and pepper to taste. Stir well, then cover and simmer for 35 minutes.

3 Add the frozen peas and mushrooms to the kettle, cover and simmer for a further 5–10 minutes, stirring occasionally, until the lentils are soft and the potatoes are cooked.
4 To serve: Taste and adjust seasoning, then transfer to a warmed shallow dish. Serve hot.

Tasty Topped Hotpots

Delicious hotpots, cooked slowly in the oven and then topped with a crispy coating are perfect one pot meals — ideal for feeding a famished family or entertaining friends.
Thinly-sliced potatoes, flavorsome biscuits, French bread croûtons, herby pastry 'cobblers' — even potato chips — make delicious, satisfying toppings which look especially appetizing when brought from the oven to the table. The humblest ingredients — from savory sausages to basic beans — can be transformed into exciting dishes when cooked in this way, as can simple, but tasty, combinations of vegetables. These satisfying hotpots are sure to be a success!

Bistro beef

Serves 4

¼ cup all-purpose flour
salt and freshly ground black pepper
1½ lb chuck steak, trimmed and cut in 1 inch cubes
2 tablespoons drippings or shortening
2 onions, sliced
1 clove garlic, minced (optional)
2 carrots, sliced
1¼ cups red wine
1¼ cups beef stock
4 tablespoons tomato paste
bouquet garni
TOPPING
4 chunky slices French bread
1–2 tablespoons Dijon mustard

1 Preheat the oven to 325°F.
2 Put the flour in a plastic bag and season with salt and pepper. Place the meat in the bag and shake until the meat is well coated with flour. Reserve any excess flour.
3 Melt the drippings in a Dutch oven, add the onions, garlic, if using, and carrots, and sauté over gentle heat for 5 minutes until the onions are lightly colored. Remove the vegetables with a slotted spoon and set aside.
4 Add the meat to the fat remaining in the pot and cook over brisk heat, turning it until browned on all sides. Return the vegetables to the pot and stir in any flour remaining from coating the meat.
5 Gradually blend in the red wine, beef stock and tomato paste. Add the bouquet garni and salt and pepper to taste.
6 Bring to a boil, stirring, then cover the pan and transfer to the oven. Cook for 2½–3 hours or until tender. Remove from the oven and discard the bouquet garni.
7 Spread the French bread with mustard and arrange, mustard side up, on top of the stew. Return to the oven, and cook, uncovered, for about 15 minutes more.

Traditional hotpot

Serves 4

4 potatoes, very thinly sliced
1½ cups thinly sliced carrots
2 onions, sliced
1 lb beef flank, trimmed of fat and cut in 1 inch cubes
2 teaspoons dried mixed herbs
salt and freshly ground black pepper
1 bay leaf
2½ cups beef stock

1 Preheat the oven to 325°F.
2 In a deep round casserole arrange layers of potatoes, carrots, onions and beef, finishing with a layer of potatoes. Sprinkle each layer with herbs and salt and pepper and add the bay leaf midway through building up the layers.
3 Pour in the stock, cover the casserole and cook in the oven for 2 hours.
4 Remove the lid and continue cooking for 15 minutes until the potato topping is light brown and all the ingredients are tender when tested by piercing them with a sharp knife. Serve the hotpot at once, straight from the casserole.

Hungarian beef pot

Serves 4–5

vegetable oil, for brushing
2 tablespoons drippings or shortening
2 lb stew beef, trimmed and cut in bite-size pieces
2 large onions, sliced
1 tablespoon mild paprika
1 celery stalk, chopped
2 cloves garlic, crushed (optional)
1 bay leaf
1 tablespoon chopped parsley
salt and freshly ground black pepper
⅔ cup red wine vinegar
4 potatoes, thinly sliced

1 Preheat the oven to 300°F and lightly brush a large ovenproof dish with oil.

2 Melt half the drippings in a heavy Dutch oven over high heat and sauté the meat in batches, if necessary, until crisp and golden on all sides. Transfer the meat with a slotted spoon to a plate.

3 Add the remaining drippings to the pot and sauté the onions gently for about 5 minutes until they are soft and translucent.

4 Return the meat and any juices to the pot. Add the paprika and stir over low heat for 2 minutes.

5 Add the celery, garlic, if using, bay leaf, parsley, salt and pepper to taste and the wine vinegar. Bring to a boil, remove from the heat and let cool for a few minutes.

6 Put half the potatoes in a layer on the bottom of the oiled ovenproof dish, cover with the meat mixture and then add the remaining potatoes in a neat layer on top. Cover tightly with a lid or foil and cook in the oven for about 2½ hours until the meat is tender when pierced with a sharp knife.

7 Brush the potatoes with oil and place the dish under a preheated hot broiler for 5 minutes until the potatoes are golden brown. Serve hot straight from the dish.

Salmon hotpot

Serves 4

1 can (16 oz) salmon, drained
2 tablespoons margarine or butter
¼ cup all-purpose flour
1¼ cups milk
1 tablespoon minced parsley
1 tablespoon tomato paste
salt and freshly ground black pepper
1 package bacon-flavored potato chips

1 Preheat the oven to 400°F.

2 Flake the salmon with a fork and then put it in a 1 quart ovenproof dish.

3 To make the sauce: Melt the margarine in a small saucepan, sprinkle in the flour and stir over low heat for 1–2 minutes until straw colored. Remove from the heat and gradually stir in the milk. Return to the heat and simmer, stirring, until thick and smooth. Stir in the parsley and tomato paste. Season to taste with salt and freshly ground black pepper.

4 Pour the sauce over the salmon and then sprinkle the potato chips over the top.

5 Bake for 15 minutes. Serve hot, straight from the dish.

Spanish beef

Serves 4

2 tablespoons olive or vegetable oil
1 onion, chopped
1 clove garlic, minced (optional)
1 lb chuck steak, cut in 1½ inch cubes
1 can (16 oz) chopped tomatoes
1 sweet red pepper, seeded and chopped
2 tablespoons medium sherry
8 stuffed green olives, halved
1 thyme sprig or ½ teaspoon dried thyme
salt and freshly ground black pepper
TOPPING
1 tablespoon butter
1 small onion, minced
1 cup long-grain rice
1¼ cups boiling water
1 tablespoon grated Parmesan cheese

1 Preheat the oven to 350°F.

2 Put olive oil in large Dutch oven, add the onion, garlic, if using, and the chuck steak and sauté for 5 minutes.

3 Add the tomatoes, half the red pepper, the sherry, green olives and thyme, and season well with salt and pepper. Bring to a boil, cover, then transfer to the oven and cook for 1¼ hours.

4 Meanwhile, make the topping: Melt the butter in a large saucepan, add the onion and sauté gently for about 5 minutes until soft.

5 Add the rice and stir until coated with butter. Add the remaining chopped red pepper and season with salt. Add the boiling water, then cover and simmer over a low heat for about 10–15 minutes, until the rice is tender and all the liquid has evaporated. Remove the rice from the heat and stir in the grated Parmesan cheese.

6 Spread the topping evenly over the meat in the pot. Return to the oven and cook, uncovered, for a further 20 minutes. Serve at once, straight from the pot.

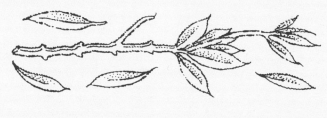

Savory sausage hotpot

Serves 4

4 tablespoons margarine or butter
2 large onions, thinly sliced
3 celery stalks, chopped
1½ lb potatoes
1 lb bulk pork sausage
1 egg, beaten
9 tablespoons dry parsley and thyme stuffing
2 tablespoons vegetable oil
1 can (8 oz) tomatoes
salt and freshly ground black pepper

1 Melt half the margarine in a large skillet, add the onions and celery and cook over moderate heat for 10–15 minutes until soft but not colored. With a slotted spoon, remove the vegetables from the skillet and place them in a layer in the bottom of a 2 quart casserole with a lid.

2 Put the potatoes into a large kettle and cover with cold water. Cover the kettle and bring to a boil. Lower the heat and simmer the potatoes for 5 minutes.

3 Meanwhile, shape the bulk sausage into 8 equal oval patties.

4 Preheat the oven to 375°F. Drain the potatoes thoroughly and let stand until cool enough to handle.

5 Roll the sausage patties first in the beaten egg, then in the dry stuffing mix, coating them thoroughly.

6 Pour the oil into the fat remaining in the skillet, add the sausage patties and cook for about 10 minutes, turning until lightly browned on all sides.

7 While the sausage patties are cooking, cut the potatoes in ¼ inch slices.

8 Arrange the browned sausage patties over the cooked vegetable mixture in the casserole. Cut the sausage patties in half if necessary so that they will fit neatly into the casserole. Break the canned tomatoes up with a fork and pour them with their juice over the sausage patties. Sprinkle with salt and pepper to taste.

9 Arrange the potato slices overlapping on top of the tomatoes and cover with the lid. Cook in the oven for 1 hour.

10 Preheat the broiler to high. Meanwhile, melt the remaining margarine. Remove the casserole lid, and brush the melted margarine over the potato topping. Place the dish under the broiler for 2–3 minutes until the potatoes are golden. Serve at once, straight from the casserole.

Sage & apple pork

Serves 4

¼ cup all-purpose flour
salt
freshly ground black pepper
½ teaspoon dried sage
1½ lb lean pork, trimmed of excess fat and cut in 1½ inch cubes
2 tablespoons butter
2 onions, thinly sliced
1½ cups diced pared Jerusalem artichokes
2 medium-size tart apples, pared, cored and sliced in ¼ inch thick rings
4–5 fresh sage leaves, if available
⅔ cup hard cider
TOPPING
1 lb potatoes, cut in pieces
2 tablespoons butter
3 tablespoons milk
1 egg yolk

1 Preheat the oven to 350°F. Put the flour in a plastic bag and season with salt and pepper and dried sage. Add the pork cubes and shake to coat them thoroughly.

2 Melt the butter in a Dutch oven and sauté the meat over moderate heat until it is browned on all sides. Remove with a slotted spoon and sauté the onion for 3 minutes, stirring often.

3 Return the meat to the pot, add the artichokes, apples and sage leaves, if using, and pour on the cider. Bring to a boil, cover the pot and cook in the oven for 1½ hours.

4 Meanwhile, to make the topping, cook the potatoes in boiling salted water until tender. Drain and mash them with the butter and milk. Season and beat in the egg yolk.

5 Stir the pork, skim off any fat from the surface, taste and adjust the seasoning, if necessary. Spread the potato over the top and fork up into peaks. Return to the oven for 20 minutes to brown.

Minted lamb hot pot

Serves 4

3 tablespoons drippings or shortening
2 lb middle neck of lamb, cut in about 12 pieces
2 onions, thinly sliced
2 cups thinly sliced carrots
¼ cup all-purpose flour
2 cups chicken stock
2 tablespoons tomato paste
5–6 teaspoons mint jelly
1 teaspoon dried mint
salt and freshly ground black pepper
2 lb potatoes, thinly sliced
1 tablespoon melted butter
a little extra dried mint

1 Preheat the oven to 325°F.
2 Melt the drippings in a large skillet. Add the lamb and sauté for a few minutes over brisk heat to brown on all sides. Drain the lamb well over the skillet, transfer to a large plate and reserve.
3 Add the onions and carrots to the skillet and sauté gently for 5 minutes until the onions are soft and lightly colored. Remove the vegetables with a slotted spoon and reserve with the lamb.
4 Sprinkle the flour into the skillet and stir over low heat for 1–2 minutes, scraping any sediment from the side and base of the skillet with a wooden spoon.
5 Blend in the stock, tomato paste, mint jelly and dried mint.
6 Bring to a boil, lower the heat and simmer for 2 minutes, stirring constantly. Season to taste with salt and pepper and remove from heat.
7 Arrange half the potato slices overlapping in the base of a large casserole. Place the lamb and vegetables on top and pour over the prepared sauce.
8 Arrange the remaining potato slices overlapping on top. Brush with the melted butter and sprinkle with a little dried mint.
9 Cover tightly with a lid or foil and cook in the oven for 2–2½ hours or until the meat and vegetables are tender when pierced with a fine skewer.
10 Increase the oven temperature to 400°F, remove the lid from the casserole and return the hotpot to the oven for 20–30 minutes or until the potato topping is golden brown.

Duck'n'beans

Serves 4

4 duck parts, each consisting of a breast and wing and weighing about
14 oz, thawed if frozen
salt and freshly ground black pepper
1 onion, chopped
1 clove garlic, minced (optional)
2 cups chicken stock
1 tablespoon medium sherry
1 jar (1 lb 2 oz) oven-baked beans
½ cup tomato sauce
½ cup fresh tomato sauce
1 tablespoon ketchup
6 oz piece of Kielbasa sausage, chopped
1 teaspoon dried thyme
1 bay leaf
TOPPING
4 tablespoons minced fresh parsley
2 cups soft white bread crumbs

1 Preheat the oven to 375°F.

2 Prick the duck parts all over with a fork, season with salt and pepper and place on a rack in a roasting pan. Roast for 1¼ hours, until the duck parts are cooked through (the juices run clear when the meat is pierced with a fine skewer). Remove the duck parts from the pan, drain on kitchen paper towels and place in a large casserole. Turn the oven temperature down to 350°F.

3 Drain off all but 1 tablespoon fat from the pan and transfer the pan to the top of the range. Add the onion and garlic, if using, and sauté gently for 2 minutes.

4 Gradually stir in the stock and sherry and bring to a boil, stirring constantly. Stir in the drained beans, the tomato sauce and ketchup, the Kielbasa sausage, thyme and bay leaf. Season to taste with salt and freshly ground black pepper.

5 Pour the mixture over the duck parts in the casserole. Cover and cook the casserole in the oven for 30 minutes.

6 Increase the oven temperature to 425°F. Mix the parsley and bread crumbs together and sprinkle evenly over the surface of the casserole. Return to the oven and cook for 15 minutes more, uncovered, to brown the herb and crumb topping. Serve hot, straight from the pot.

Kidney carbonnade

Serves 4

1¼ lb lamb kidneys, halved and cores removed
5 tablespoons margarine or butter
2 onions, thinly sliced
1 cup halved button mushrooms
¼ cup all-purpose flour
1¼ cups beer
1 tablespoon tomato paste
½ teaspoon dried thyme
pinch of sugar
pinch of freshly grated nutmeg
salt and freshly ground black pepper
TOPPING
½ small French bread stick, cut in ½ inch slices
1½–2 tablespoons Dijon mustard
2 tablespoons minced fresh parsley, for garnish

1 Preheat the oven to 350°F. Rinse the kidneys under cold running water and then pat them dry with kitchen paper towels.

2 Melt 4 tablespoons of the margarine in a saucepan, add the onions and cook gently for 5 minutes, stirring occasionally, until lightly colored. Add the kidneys and mushrooms and cook over brisk heat for 3–4 minutes, stirring, until the kidneys are evenly browned. Using a slotted spoon, transfer the browned kidneys and the vegetables to a casserole.

3 Melt the remaining margarine in the pan, sprinkle in the flour and then stir over low heat for 1–2 minutes. Gradually stir in the beer, then the tomato paste, thyme, sugar and nutmeg and season to taste with salt and pepper. Bring the mixture slowly to a boil, stirring constantly, then lower the heat and simmer gently for 2 minutes. Pour the mixture over the kidneys and stir carefully.

4 For the topping, spread the slices of bread with the mustard, then arrange them mustard side up in a circle around the kidneys.

5 Cook, uncovered, in the oven for 30 minutes, until the bread slices are golden brown and crunchy. Sprinkle top with the parsley and serve at once, straight from the casserole.

Liver cobbler

Serves 4

¾ lb lamb liver, cut in bite-size pieces
1¼ cups milk
1 tablespoon all-purpose flour
salt and freshly ground black pepper
¼ cup margarine or butter
6 bacon slices, cut in thin strips
2 large onions, sliced
1 can (8 oz) tomatoes
½ teaspoon dried mixed herbs
TOPPING
2 cups self-rising flour
pinch of salt
¼ cup diced margarine or butter
½ teaspoon dried mixed herbs
⅔ cup milk
a little milk, for glaze

1 Put the liver pieces in a shallow dish, pour over the milk and marinate at room temperature for 1 hour.

2 Remove the liver from the milk and dry on kitchen paper towels. Spread out the flour on a flat plate and season with salt and pepper. Dip the liver in the flour to coat thoroughly.

3 Melt the margarine in a skillet, add the bacon and onions and sauté gently for 5 minutes until soft. Remove with a slotted spoon and put in a round 1½ quart casserole, 9 inches in diameter.

4 Add the liver to the skillet and sauté for 1–2 minutes to seal.

5 Gradually stir the milk into the pan and bring to a boil, stirring. Cook for 2–3 minutes.

6 Using a slotted spoon, transfer the liver to the casserole with the onions and bacon. Pour in the milk and stir in the tomatoes with their juice and the herbs. Season to taste.

7 Preheat the oven to 425°F.

8 Make the cobbler topping: Sift the flour and salt into a bowl. Cut in the margarine and rub it into the flour until the mixture resembles fine bread crumbs. Add the herbs and gradually mix in the milk to form a soft dough.

9 Place the dough on a lightly floured working surface and knead gently until smooth. Roll out to ½ inch thick. Use a 2½ inch cutter to cut rounds.

10 Arrange the rounds of dough overlapping in a circle on top of the liver mixture in the casserole. Brush the topping with a little milk to glaze.

11 Bake the cobbler in the oven for 20–25 minutes until the topping is well risen and golden brown. Serve at once, straight from the casserole.

Rustic bean pot

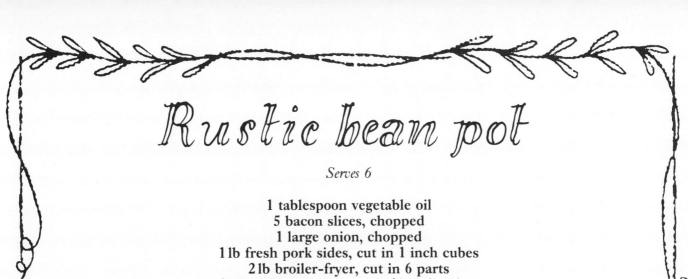

Serves 6

1 tablespoon vegetable oil
5 bacon slices, chopped
1 large onion, chopped
1 lb fresh pork sides, cut in 1 inch cubes
2 lb broiler-fryer, cut in 6 parts
½ lb garlic sausage, cut in ½ inch cubes
1¼ cups dried navy beans, soaked in cold water overnight and drained
4 cups chicken stock
1½ cups chopped peeled tomatoes
bouquet garni
salt and freshly ground black pepper
2 cups soft white bread crumbs

1 Preheat the oven to 325°F.

2 Heat the oil in a large Dutch oven, add the bacon and onion and sauté gently for 5 minutes until the onion is soft and lightly colored.

3 Increase the heat slightly, add the pork cubes and sauté for about 6 minutes, turning until lightly browned on all sides. Using a slotted spoon, transfer the bacon, onion and pork to a bowl and set aside.

4 Add the chicken parts to the fat remaining in the pot and cook for about 5 minutes, stirring until browned on all sides. Pour off the fat from the pot, leaving the chicken parts in the pot.

5 Add the reserved bacon, onion and pork to the pot together with the garlic sausage, drained beans, stock, tomatoes, bouquet garni and salt and pepper to taste. Stir to mix well, then bring to a boil. Cover the pot and cook in the oven for 1½ hours.

6 Remove and discard the bouquet garni. Sprinkle the mixture with bread crumbs and cook uncovered for 1 further hour until the top is crisp and lightly browned. Serve at once, straight from the pot.

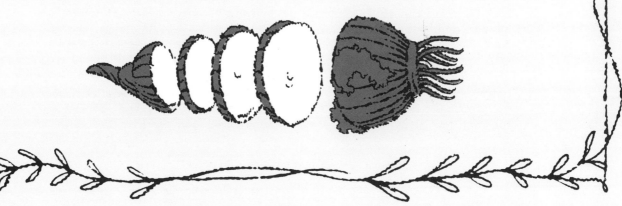

Goober cobbler

Serves 4

2 small turnips, cut in 1 inch cubes
salt
1 lb potatoes, cut in 1 inch chunks
¼ cup margarine or butter
1 onion, finely sliced
1 cup sliced mushrooms
⅓ cup all-purpose flour
⅔ cup chicken stock
1¼ cups milk
1 cup shredded Cheddar cheese
freshly ground black pepper
3 tomatoes, peeled and quartered
TOPPING
1½ cups wholewheat flour
1 tablespoon baking powder
½ teaspoon salt
3 tablespoons diced margarine
2 tablespoons finely chopped roasted peanuts
¾ teaspoon dried mixed herbs
about ⅔ cup milk

1 Place the turnips in a large saucepan of salted water and bring to a boil. Lower the heat and simmer for 5 minutes. Add the potatoes, return to a boil, then lower the heat again and simmer for 10 minutes more until the vegetables are just tender. Drain and reserve.

2 Melt the margarine in a saucepan, add the onion and sauté gently for 5 minutes until soft and lightly colored. Add the mushrooms and continue cooking for 5 minutes. Transfer the vegetables to a plate with a slotted spoon.

3 Sprinkle the flour into the pan and stir over low heat for 1–2 minutes. Remove from the heat and gradually stir in the stock and the milk. Return to the heat and simmer, stirring, until the sauce is thick and smooth. Reserve 1 tablespoon of the cheese and stir the rest into the sauce. Season to taste with salt and freshly ground black pepper.

4 Stir in the turnips, potatoes, onion and mushrooms and tomatoes. Taste and adjust the seasoning, then put the vegetable mixture into a 3 quart casserole.

5 Preheat the oven to 425°F.

6 Make the biscuit topping: Sift the flour, baking powder and salt into a large bowl. Tip the bran left in the sifter into the bowl and stir well to mix. Cut in the margarine and rub it in with the fingertips until the mixture resembles fine bread crumbs. Add the peanuts and herbs and gradually mix in enough milk to form a soft dough.

7 Put the dough onto a lightly floured working surface and roll out thinly. Cut in about 15 rounds using a 2 inch cutter and arrange these on top of the casserole. Sprinkle with the reserved cheese.

8 Bake the casserole in the oven for about 30 minutes or until the biscuit topping has risen and is golden brown. Serve at once.

Cauliflower, mushroom & oat crisp

Serves 6–8

3 cups cauliflower flowerets
salt and freshly ground black pepper
2 tablespoons all-purpose flour
1¼ cups dairy sour cream
1 teaspoon mild yellow mustard
1½ cups shredded Monterey Jack
½ lb button mushrooms, trimmed
2 tablespoons butter
1 cup rolled oats
½ cup roughly chopped walnuts

1 Preheat the oven to 400°F. Drop the cauliflower flowerets in a saucepan containing 1 inch of boiling salted water and cook for about 7 minutes, or until they are just tender; drain well.

2 Meanwhile, put the flour in a small bowl and blend to a smooth paste with a little of the sour cream. Gradually stir in the remaining sour cream, the mustard, half the shredded cheese and salt and black pepper to taste.

3 Mix in the cauliflower and mushrooms, turning gently so that all the vegetables are coated. Spoon into a shallow ovenproof dish.

4 Using a fork, mix the butter with the oats, then add the rest of the cheese and the walnuts to make a lumpy, crumbly mixture. Sprinkle evenly over the cauliflower and mushrooms and bake for 40 minutes, until the topping is golden and crisp. Serve at once.

Succulent Pot Roasts

Pot roasting is one of the most successful ways of cooking large joints of meat or whole birds. Simmered gently with a combination of vegetables, herbs and stock the meat emerges from the pot juicy and tender, while the accompanying sauce is full of natural goodness. Making use of the whole piece of meat, pot roasted dishes are excellent for entertaining – an exciting alternative to meat traditionally roasted in the oven, and an easier dish to prepare.

Pot roasted dishes range from traditional sides of ham cooked with split peas and root vegetables to sophisticated rolled beef, stuffed with walnuts and mushrooms. Whatever the occasion you are cooking for – whether Sunday lunch or midweek supper – you are sure to find the perfect dish among these pot roasts!

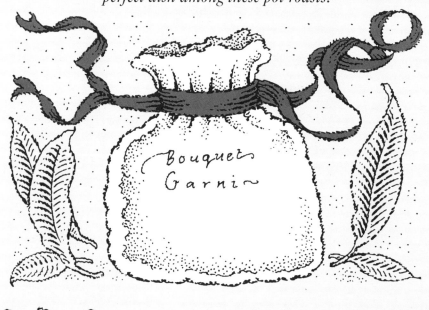

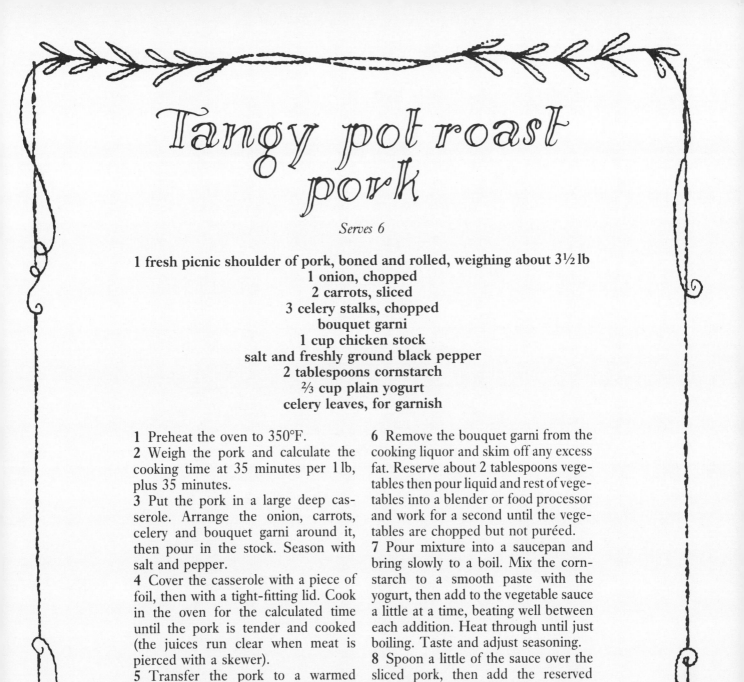

Tangy pot roast pork

Serves 6

1 fresh picnic shoulder of pork, boned and rolled, weighing about 3½ lb
1 onion, chopped
2 carrots, sliced
3 celery stalks, chopped
bouquet garni
1 cup chicken stock
salt and freshly ground black pepper
2 tablespoons cornstarch
⅔ cup plain yogurt
celery leaves, for garnish

1 Preheat the oven to 350°F.
2 Weigh the pork and calculate the cooking time at 35 minutes per 1 lb, plus 35 minutes.
3 Put the pork in a large deep casserole. Arrange the onion, carrots, celery and bouquet garni around it, then pour in the stock. Season with salt and pepper.
4 Cover the casserole with a piece of foil, then with a tight-fitting lid. Cook in the oven for the calculated time until the pork is tender and cooked (the juices run clear when meat is pierced with a skewer).
5 Transfer the pork to a warmed carving dish, remove any string, strip off the rind and fat and carve the pork in neat slices. Arrange on a warmed serving platter, cover and keep hot in the oven turned to its lowest setting.

6 Remove the bouquet garni from the cooking liquor and skim off any excess fat. Reserve about 2 tablespoons vegetables then pour liquid and rest of vegetables into a blender or food processor and work for a second until the vegetables are chopped but not puréed.
7 Pour mixture into a saucepan and bring slowly to a boil. Mix the cornstarch to a smooth paste with the yogurt, then add to the vegetable sauce a little at a time, beating well between each addition. Heat through until just boiling. Taste and adjust seasoning.
8 Spoon a little of the sauce over the sliced pork, then add the reserved vegetables to the platter and spoon a little sauce over them. Garnish with celery leaves. Serve the sliced pork and vegetables at once with the remaining sauce passed separately.

Two-in-one ham

Serves 6–8

3–3½ lb country-cured ham roast
1 cup dried split peas
1 large onion, chopped
1 bay leaf
salt and freshly ground black pepper
1 lb potatoes, quartered
1 lb carrots, cut in 2 inch sticks
1 lb leeks, cut in ¾ inch slices
PARSLEY SAUCE
3 tablespoons margarine or butter
⅓ cup all-purpose flour
⅔ cup milk
⅔ cup light cream
4 tablespoons chopped fresh parsley
SOUP GARNISH
⅔ cup light cream
fried bread croutons

1 Put the ham in a large bowl, add the split peas and cover with cold water. Cover the bowl, then let soak in a cool place for about 8 hours or overnight.
2 Lift out the ham and place in a large kettle. Drain the soaked peas, rinse under cold running water, then add to the kettle with the onion and bay leaf.
3 Pour about 9 cups cold water into the kettle to cover the ham and bring to a boil. Skim off any foam, then lower the heat, cover and simmer for 1¼ hours until the peas are soft.
4 Remove the ham from the kettle, place on a plate and set aside. Pour the stock through a strainer into a large liquid measure.
5 Make the soup: Discard the bay leaf from the peas and onion left in the strainer, then put the peas and onion in a blender or food processor. Add 5 cups of the stock to the blender or processor and work the mixture until smooth in batches, if necessary.
6 Pour the puréed soup into a large saucepan, season to taste with salt and pepper and set aside.
7 Remove the skin from the reserved ham roast and return to the rinsed and dried kettle. Add the potatoes, carrots and leeks to the kettle and pour in 2½ cups of the remaining ham stock.
8 Cover the kettle, bring back to a boil, lower the heat and simmer for about 20 minutes until the vegetables are tender.
9 Meanwhile, make the sauce: Melt the margarine in a saucepan, sprinkle in the flour and stir over low heat for 1–2 minutes until straw-colored. Off

heat, gradually stir in the remaining stock and milk. Return to the heat and simmer, stirring, until thick and smooth. Stir in the cream and parsley, season to taste with salt and pepper and heat through gently for 2 minutes. Set aside.

10 Put the pot of soup over low heat and heat through gently.

11 Remove the ham from the kettle and place on a warmed serving platter. Remove the vegetables from the kettle with a slotted spoon and arrange around the ham. Keep hot in a pre-heated 325°F oven.

12 To serve the split pea soup, pour it into individual warmed soup bowls, and garnish as follows: Swirl cream into each and top with croutons. Serve the split pea soup at once as a first course.

13 Just before serving the ham, reheat the parsley sauce and transfer to a warmed sauceboat. Serve the ham carved into slices, with the vegetables and parsley sauce.

Ham, beans & apple

Serves 4–6

3–3½ lb smoked ham shoulder butt
1½ cups navy beans
1 lb leeks, sliced
2 large tart apples, pared, cored and chopped
2 bay leaves
freshly ground black pepper
3 tablespoons butter
¼ cup all-purpose flour
⅔ cup unsweetened apple juice
1 tablespoon light brown sugar
chopped fresh parsley, for garnish

1 Put the ham and the navy beans in separate bowls and pour over enough cold water to cover. Cover the bowls and let ham and beans soak in a cool place, preferably the refrigerator, for about 8 hours or overnight.

2 Transfer the ham to a large kettle. Drain the soaked beans, rinse under cold running water, then add to the kettle with the leeks, apples and bay leaves. Season with black pepper.

3 Pour fresh cold water into the kettle to cover the ham and bring to a boil. Skim off any foam, lower the heat, cover and simmer for 2–2½ hours or until beans are soft.

4 Preheat the oven to 225°F.

5 Using 2 fish turners, transfer the ham to a plate and remove the skin. Strain the stock and reserve 1¼ cups.

Discard the bay leaves and transfer beans, apples and leeks to a serving dish. Dot the bean mixture with 1 tablespoon butter. Cover both plate and dish and keep warm in the oven.

6 Melt the remaining butter in a saucepan. Sprinkle over the flour and cook for 1–2 minutes until straw-colored. Gradually stir in the reserved stock and the apple juice. Bring to a boil, then lower the heat and simmer for 3 minutes, stirring, until smooth. Stir in the sugar and season with freshly ground black pepper.

7 Carve the ham in slices, then arrange on a warmed serving platter and pour over the sauce. Sprinkle with chopped parsley and serve at once, with the bean, apple and leek mixture passed separately.

New England dinner

Serves 6–8

4½ lb piece corned beef
1 medium onion, halved
bouquet garni
8 medium carrots
4 small white turnips, quartered
8 medium potatoes, quartered
1 tablespoon dark brown sugar
salt and freshly ground black pepper
8 pearl onions, peeled and left whole
1 small cabbage heart, cut in wedges
8 small beets, cooked, peeled and quartered
1 tablespoon chopped parsley, for garnish

1 Put the beef into a large kettle. Cover with cold water and bring to a boil, then drain and discard the liquid.

2 Return the meat to the rinsed-out kettle, cover with cold water again, then add the onion halves and the bouquet garni. Bring to a boil again. Using a skimmer or slotted spoon, skim off the foam as it rises to the surface. Cover the kettle and simmer over low heat for 2½ hours.

3 Off heat, discard the onion and bouquet garni. Add the carrots, turnips, potatoes, sugar and salt and pepper, and bring back to a boil. Lower the heat, cover the pan and simmer again for a further 30 minutes.

4 Add the whole onions and the cabbage, return to a boil, lower the heat and simmer for a further 15 minutes, or until the meat and all the vegetables are tender.

5 Meanwhile, put the beets in a steamer or in a metal colander over a saucepan half filled with boiling water. Cook for 15 minutes.

6 Transfer the meat to a warmed carving dish and surround with the beets and a few of the other vegetables to garnish. Keep hot.

7 With a slotted spoon transfer the remaining vegetables to a warmed serving dish and keep hot while you make the sauce.

8 Skim the excess fat from the top of the cooking liquid with a skimmer or bulb baster. Bring the liquid quickly to a boil and boil briskly for 3–5 minutes to reduce the volume. Taste and adjust seasoning.

9 Just before serving, garnish the vegetables with the parsley and pour the sauce into a warmed sauceboat to pass separately.

Slow-cooked beef & sauerkraut

Serves 6

3 tablespoons drippings or shortening
3–3½ lb boneless beef brisket, tied in a compact shape
1 onion, chopped
1 tart apple, pared and sliced
1 lb sauerkraut
1 tablespoon juniper berries, lightly crushed
2½ cups hot beef stock
salt and freshly ground black pepper
2 tablespoons tomato paste
¼ cup dairy sour cream

1 Melt the drippings over moderate heat in a Dutch oven large enough to take the vegetables and the beef. When the fat is very hot, add the beef and turn to brown on all sides. Remove the beef from the pot and set aside. Pour away all but 2 tablespoons of the fat in the pot.

2 Add the onion and apple to the pot and stir to coat with the hot fat. Place the brisket on top of this mixture and add the sauerkraut and juniper berries. Pour over the hot beef stock and bring to a boil. Season to taste with salt and pepper.

3 Cover the Dutch oven, lower the heat and simmer for 2½ hours, turning the beef once during this time and stirring the vegetables occasionally.

4 Remove the beef, discard the string and carve into slices. Blot the excess fat from the surface of the sauerkraut mixture, using kitchen paper towels. With a slotted spoon transfer the sauerkraut, apple and juniper berry mixture to a large warmed serving platter. Arrange the sliced beef down the center of the platter and keep warm in a preheated 325°F oven.

5 Strain the cooking liquor into a clean saucepan and stir in the tomato paste. Bring to a boil and cook until reduced to around 2 cups.

6 Stir the sour cream into the sauce. Drizzle a little of the sauce down the center of the sliced beef and pass the rest separately in a sauceboat. Serve the beef immediately.

Beef & eggplant braise

Serves 4

1½ lb eggplant, cut in ¾ inch cubes
salt
2 lb top round of beef, rolled and tied
3 tablespoons vegetable oil
3 onions, chopped
1 clove garlic, crushed
1 carrot, thinly sliced
1 can (16 oz) chopped tomatoes
freshly ground black pepper

1 Put the eggplant cubes in a colander, sprinkle with salt, put a plate on top and weight down. Let drain for about 30 minutes to remove the bitter juices.

2 Pat the beef dry on kitchen paper towels. Heat the oil in a large heavy-bottomed Dutch oven or kettle. Add the beef and cook for 2–3 minutes, turning meat once or twice, to brown and seal on all sides. Drain the beef over the pan and set aside on a plate.

3 Add the onions and garlic to the pot and cook gently for 5 minutes until soft and lightly colored. Add the carrot, stir well and cook for a further 1 minute.

4 Rinse the eggplant cubes under cold running water, pat dry and add to the pan. Add the chopped tomatoes with their juice, season with salt and pepper and stir well.

5 Return the beef to the Dutch oven or kettle and cover tightly with the lid. Cook the beef and vegetables very gently for about 2½ hours or until the meat is cooked to your liking.

6 Transfer the beef to a warmed serving platter. With the vegetables still in the pan, taste them and adjust the seasoning if necessary. Carve the beef in neat slices and spoon the vegetables around the meat on the serving platter. Serve at once.

Walnut~stuffed brisket

Serves 4

2½ lb piece boneless beef brisket
2 tablespoons vegetable oil
1 onion, sliced
2 celery stalks, chopped
2 carrots, thinly sliced
1 tablespoon tomato paste
1 cup beef or chicken stock

FILLING

3 tablespoons margarine or butter
1 onion, minced
½ cup finely chopped mushrooms
2 tablespoons soft white bread crumbs
⅓ cup chopped walnuts
salt and freshly ground black pepper

1 Preheat the oven to 350°F.

2 Make the filling: Melt the margarine in a small saucepan, add the onion and sauté gently for 5 minutes until soft and lightly colored. Add the mushrooms and cook for 5 minutes. Off heat, stir in the bread crumbs and walnuts and season to taste with salt and pepper.

3 Place the brisket flat on a board and spread the filling evenly over it, to within 1 inch of the edge. Press the filling down with the back of a spoon. Roll up from one of the short edges, pressing the meat down gently as you roll, to keep the filling in place. Tie the rolled brisket in several places with fine string.

4 Heat the oil in a Dutch oven. Add the sliced onion and celery and sauté over moderate heat for 2 minutes, stirring once or twice. Add the carrots, stir and sauté for 1 minute more, then add the tomato paste and stock and season carefully with salt and pepper. Bring to a boil, stirring, then add the beef.

5 Cover the pot, transfer to the oven and cook for 2½ hours, or until the juices run clear when the brisket is pierced with a sharp knife.

6 Transfer the brisket to a warmed serving platter and remove the string. Remove the vegetables from the pot with a slotted spoon and arrange them around the brisket. Strain the cooking liquid.

7 Carve the meat in slices and serve hot, with the strained liquor passed separately in a warmed pitcher.

Beef with creamy wine sauce

Serves 4

3 tablespoons shortening
2 lb rolled top round of beef
2 cups sliced carrots
2 cups sliced scallions
8 cloves
1 onion, quartered
⅔ cup red wine
¼ cup water
⅔ cup dairy sour cream
¼ teaspoon ground allspice
salt and freshly ground black pepper

1 Preheat the oven to 325°F.
2 Melt the shortening over moderate heat in a Dutch oven large enough to take the vegetables and the beef. When the shortening is very hot, add the beef and turn to brown on all sides. Remove the beef from the pot and set aside. Pour away all but 2 tablespoons of the fat in the pot.
3 Add the carrots and scallions to the pot and stir, coating the vegetables evenly with the hot fat.
4 Put the browned beef on top of the vegetables. Stick 2 cloves into each onion quarter and arrange them around the beef.
5 Add the red wine and water to the pot and bring to a boil. Transfer to the oven and cook for 1½ hours, turning the meat once.
6 Remove the beef, discard the string and carve in slices. Remove the vegetables with a slotted spoon and put them on a warmed serving platter. Arrange the sliced beef on top. Keep hot in lowest possible oven.
7 Boil the cooking liquid in the pot rapidly for about 5 minutes, until reduced slightly. Off heat, stir in the sour cream and allspice. Season to taste with salt and pepper. Heat through very gently, but do not allow to boil. Pour a little of the sauce over the beef, then serve at once, with the remaining sauce passed separately in a warmed sauceboat.

Lamb & cider pot roast

Serves 4

2 tablespoons drippings or shortening
2½–3 lb knuckle end leg of lamb
1 onion stuck with 4 cloves
½ lb carrots, quartered lengthwise
½ lb parsnips, quartered lengthwise
½ lb turnips, quartered
2 potatoes, cut in chunks
⅔ cup hard cider
⅔ cup chicken stock
salt and freshly ground black pepper
BEURRE MANIÉ (kneaded butter)
2 tablespoons all-purpose flour
2 tablespoons butter

1 Preheat the oven to 325°F.
2 Melt the drippings in a Dutch oven over moderate heat. Add the lamb and brown on all sides.
3 Add the vegetables to the pot, pour in cider and stock. Season to taste with salt and pepper.
4 Cover the pot and cook in the oven for 2–2¼ hours or until the lamb is cooked through (the juices run clear when the meat is pierced with a skewer).
5 Transfer the lamb to a warmed serving platter. Using a slotted spoon, lift out all the vegetables and arrange them around the meat, discarding the onion. Keep hot in oven turned to its lowest setting.
6 Make the beurre manié: Mix flour and butter together with a round-bladed knife to make a paste, then cut the paste in pea-size pieces.
7 Bring the cooking liquid in the pot to a boil, then beat in the pieces of beurre manié. Simmer over low heat, beating constantly, until the gravy thickens. Taste and adjust seasoning, if necessary. Pour the gravy into a warmed gravy boat.
8 Carve the lamb in slices. Serve immediately, with the gravy passed separately.

Saucy lamb

Serves 4–6

3 lb leg of lamb
⅔ cup red wine
⅔ cup water
1 tablespoon white wine vinegar
1 medium onion, minced
1 teaspoon dried oregano
2 tablespoons vegetable oil
2 tablespoons tomato paste
pinch of sugar
salt and freshly ground black pepper
chopped parsley, for garnish

1 Put the lamb into a large bowl. Mix together the wine, water, vinegar, onion and oregano and pour over the lamb. Cover and leave to marinate in the refrigerator for several hours, preferably overnight. Turn the lamb in the marinade from time to time.

2 Remove the lamb and reserve the marinade. Pat the lamb all over with kitchen paper towels until dry.

3 Heat the oil in a large Dutch oven, add the lamb and cook over moderate heat until browned on all sides. Pour over the reserved marinade and cover the pot with a tight-fitting lid. Cook over low heat for 1½–2 hours or until the meat is cooked to your liking.

4 Remove the lamb and keep hot. Draw off any fat from the cooking liquor with a bulb baster, then stir in the tomato paste and sugar.

5 Bring the cooking liquor to a boil, add salt and pepper to taste, then lower the heat and return the lamb to the pot. Simmer gently for 5 minutes more.

6 To serve, transfer the lamb to a warmed serving dish, pour over the sauce and sprinkle with parsley. Serve at once.

Chicken with endive

Serves 6

**3½ lb broiler-fryer, with liver
1 clove garlic, crushed
2 onions, finely chopped
salt and freshly ground black pepper
2 tablespoons butter
2 lb Belgian endive, chopped
freshly grated nutmeg**

1 Chop the chicken liver finely, then mix with crushed garlic and one-third of the chopped onion. Season with salt and pepper to taste. Stuff the chicken with the mixture and truss it with string.

2 Melt the butter in a large Dutch oven, add the chicken and sauté over moderate heat, turning occasionally, until browned all over. Drain well over the pot and keep hot.

3 Add the remaining chopped onion and the chopped endive to the pot. Cover, turn the heat to low and sweat over very low heat for 10 minutes.

4 Season the endive with a little nutmeg and salt and pepper to taste. Add the chicken, cover and cook very gently for about 1 hour or until the chicken is tender.

5 Transfer the chicken to a warmed serving platter, remove string and keep hot. Increase the heat and stir until the moisture on the endive has reduced to a glaze. Arrange the endive around the chicken and serve.

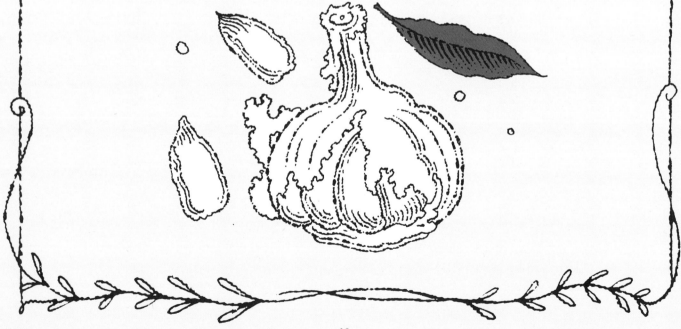

Rum chicken

Serves 4–6

3–3½ lb broiler-fryer
2 tablespoons margarine or butter
1 tablespoon vegetable oil
4 bacon slices, chopped
½ lb pearl onions
¼ cup dark rum
bouquet garni
2½ cups chicken stock
1 teaspoon soy sauce
1 teaspoon Worcestershire sauce
½ lb button mushrooms
3 jars (2 oz each) chopped pimientos, drained
salt and freshly ground black pepper

1 Pat the chicken dry with kitchen paper towels.

2 Heat the margarine and oil in a large Dutch oven, add the chicken and cook over moderate heat, turning occasionally, until browned all over. Drain well over the pot and set aside.

3 Put the bacon and onions in the Dutch oven and sauté over moderate heat for 5 minutes, stirring the mixture occasionally.

4 Remove the pot from the heat and return the chicken to it. Warm the rum over gentle heat in a small saucepan. Remove from the heat, ignite with a match, then pour over the chicken.

5 Add the bouquet garni, stock, soy sauce and Worcestershire to the pot. Cover and simmer the mixture gently for 45 minutes.

6 Add the mushrooms and pimientos and continue cooking for 15–20 minutes or until the chicken is cooked through (the juices run clear when the flesh is pierced in the thickest part with a skewer).

7 Meanwhile, preheat the oven to 225°F.

8 Carefully transfer the chicken to a warmed serving dish. Remove the vegetables with a slotted spoon and arrange around the chicken. Keep hot in the oven.

9 Skim the fat from the liquid in the pot and discard the bouquet garni. Taste the sauce and adjust seasoning if necessary. Pour into a warmed sauceboat.

10 Serve the chicken carved into slices; pass sauce separately.

Chicken with parsley dumplings

Serves 4–6

5–5½ lb stewing hen or capon, cleaned, with giblets
½ lemon
1 ham shank
2 large onions, sliced
2 carrots, sliced
2 celery stalks, sliced
1 teaspoon salt
6–8 whole black peppercorns
a few parsley stalks
parsley sprigs, for garnish
DUMPLINGS
1 cup self-rising flour
¼ teaspoon salt
¼ cup chopped beef suet
1 tablespoon minced fresh parsley
about ¼ cup milk
SAUCE
2 tablespoons margarine
¼ cup all-purpose flour
⅔ cup milk

1 Wipe the chicken inside and out with kitchen paper towels, then rub the skin all over with the cut lemon.

2 Put the chicken into a very large kettle with the giblets (discarding the liver), the ham shank and the remaining ingredients except the parsley sprigs. Pour in just enough cold water to cover the chicken, bring slowly to a boil, then skim off any foam that rises to the surface with a bulb baster. Lower the heat, cover the kettle and simmer for 3½–4 hours until the chicken is cooked and really tender.

3 Meanwhile, make the dumplings: Sift the flour and salt into a bowl and add the suet and parsley. Make a well in the center and add a little milk. Gradually work the dry ingredients into the center adding just enough milk to make a firm dough. Divide the dough into 8 pieces and roll each into a ball with floured hands.

4 When the chicken and ham shank have been simmering for about 3¼ hours, transfer the ham shank to a

board. Increase the heat under the kettle, bring to a boil, then add the dumplings to the kettle and cook for 20 minutes more.

5 Preheat the oven to 225°F.

6 Meanwhile, cut the meat from the ham shank, discarding excess fat, cut into bite-size pieces and reserve.

7 Remove the kettle from the heat. Lift the chicken from the kettle and drain it thoroughly. Pat dry with kitchen paper towels and then place on a warmed serving platter. Remove the dumplings and arrange around the chicken. Keep hot in the oven.

8 Strain the cooking liquor left in the kettle and measure 1¼ cups.

9 Make the sauce: Melt the margarine in a small saucepan, sprinkle in the flour and stir over low heat for 1–2 minutes until straw-colored. Off heat, gradually stir in the milk and measured cooking liquor. Return to the heat and simmer, stirring, until thick and smooth. Stir in diced ham.

10 Spoon a little of the sauce over the chicken and garnish with parsley sprigs. Serve at once, with the remaining sauce passed separately in a warmed sauceboat.

Braised lamb with vegetables

Serves 4

3 lb lamb shoulder
1 lb potatoes, quartered
2 cups sliced carrots
2 cups sliced onions
1¼ cups chicken stock
1 clove garlic, minced (optional)
salt and freshly ground black pepper

1 Preheat the oven to 400°F.

2 Put the lamb in a large casserole and arrange the potatoes, carrots and onions around the meat.

3 Pour over the stock and add the garlic, if using. Season with salt and pepper to taste.

4 Cover the casserole with a piece of foil, then with a tight-fitting lid. Cook in the oven for 1 hour, then remove the foil and lid and cook for a further 45 minutes until nicely browned.

5 Transfer the lamb to a warmed serving platter. Remove the vegetables from the casserole with a slotted spoon and arrange them around the lamb. Strain the cooking liquor.

6 Carve the meat in slices and serve hot with the strained liquor handed separately in a warmed pitcher.

63

Index